2

1

INVENTOR'S SECRET SCRAPBOOK

Chris Oxlade

Published 2010 by
A&C Black Publishers Ltd.
36 Soho Square, London, W1D 3QY

www.acblack.com

ISBN 978-1-4081-2439-0

Series consultant: Gill Matthews

Text copyright © 2010 Chris Oxlade

A CIP catalogue for this book is available from the British Library.

This book is produced using paper that is made from wood grown in managed, sustainable forests. It is natural,
renewable and recyclable. The logging and manufacturing processes conform to the environmental regulations of
the country of origin.

Produced for A&C Black by Calcium. www.calciumcreative.co.uk

Printed and bound in China by C&C Offset Printing Co.

All the internet addresses given in this book were correct at the time of going to press. The author and
publishers regret any inconvenience caused if addresses have changed or sites have ceased to exist, but can
accept no responsibility for any such changes.

Acknowledgements

The publishers would like to thank the following for their kind permission to reproduce their photographs:

Cover: Shutterstock. **Pages:** Istockphoto: Catherine Yeulet 22t; Library of Congress: 10, 12t, 14t, 14b, 16t, 16b,
20t, 20b; NASA: 4, 24t, 24b; Shutterstock: 3d brained 22b, Eugene Berman 26, C 5b, David Davis 29b, James
Hoenstine 12b, Jakub Krechowicz 5t, Tim Jenner 11, Massimiliano Lamagna 8, Galushko Sergey 18, Sgame 6b,
Alex Staroseltsev 29t; Wikimedia Commons: Enrique Dans 28, Wouter Hagens 6t, Royal Air Force 27

CONTENTS

All About Inventing...4

The Microscope..6

The Electric Motor...8

A Calculator Machine..10

The Electric Light Bulb.......................................12

The Telephone..14

The Wireless Telegraph.......................................16

The Vacuum Cleaner...18

A Flying Machine..20

The Television..22

The Rocket..24

The Jet Engine...26

The World Wide Web..28

Glossary..30

Further Information...31

Index..32

ALL ABOUT INVENTING

Inside this book you'll find pages of scraps from the notebooks of some of the world's greatest inventors. Discover how they came up with their incredible ideas – from the humble light bulb to a fantastic flying machine.

Read on and perhaps you'll get an idea for your own invention – if you do, be sure to make a record of it in your own inventor's scrapbook.

INVENTORS AND INVENTING

Humans have been inventing for tens of thousands of years. They started by inventing simple tools for hunting and preparing food, made from materials they found around them.

Think of inventing and you might imagine a boffin in a white coat having a sudden and brilliant idea! Some inventions happen like this – but not many. Most are the result of years of painstaking work, making working models, testing them and making yet more working models.

Inventions have made space travel possible.

The greatest inventor

The Italian Leonardo da Vinci (1452–1519) was probably the greatest inventor of all time. He filled notebooks with sketches of amazing machines. He invented a parachute, a helicopter, a tank, and even a submarine – but could build none of them with the **technology** of the time.

The importance of patents

A patent is a sort of agreement made between an inventor and the government of a country. An inventor always tries to patent an invention. It protects the inventor's idea from being pinched by someone else – normally for about 20 years.

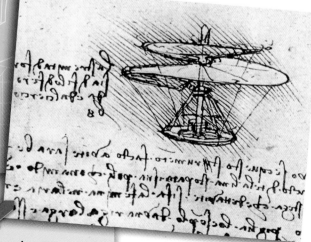

Leonardo even sketched out an idea for an early helicopter.

THE MICROSCOPE

INVENTOR: ANTON VAN LEEUWENHOEK

It's a very exciting time! I've discovered how to make a **microscope** using tiny glass **lenses** that I make myself at home. It's brilliant because peering through my microscope I've seen lots of tiny animals that I couldn't see before. I've decided to call them 'animalcules'. I'm sure nobody even knew these creatures existed before. What a discovery!

Anton van Leeuwenhoek

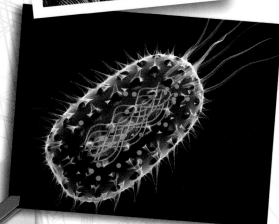

The microscope allowed Leeuwenhoek to see tiny bugs for the first time.

TIMELINE

1590 The first microscopes are made in Holland by spectacle makers Zacharias Janssen and Hans Lippershey

1660s Robert Hooke (Britain) publishes a book of his observations through his own microscope

HOW A MICROSCOPE IS MADE Anton Van Leeuwenhoek

1 The end of a thin strand of glass is put into a hot flame. The glass melts, making tiny glass balls. These balls become the lenses of the microscopes.

2 Two metal pieces are made. Each has a small hole in the centre slightly smaller than a lens (prepared in step 1). The pieces are pressed together, trapping the lens between the holes.

3 A metal pin is fixed on one side of the microscope. The sharp point of the pin is in line with the lens.

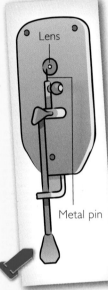

Lens

Metal pin

To use the microscope:

- the object that is to be studied is stuck on the pin
- the user holds the microscope close to his or her eye and looks through the lens
- the position of the pin is changed until the specimen can be seen clearly

This type of microscope can show things at 200 times their normal size.

DID YOU KNOW?

Anton van Leeuwenhoek did not actually invent the first microscope. Microscopes had been around for twenty or thirty years by the time he began making his microscopes. But he perfected a way of making lenses that produced very clear images – and he kept it top secret.

1675 Anton van Leeuwenhoek discovers **micro-organisms** by looking through his single-lens microscopes

1938 Ernst Ruska (Germany) develops the **electron microscope**, which allows much greater detail to be seen than with an optical microscope*

a microscope that uses light to magnify things

THE ELECTRIC MOTOR
INVENTOR: MICHAEL FARADAY

Electricity is the buzzword of the moment. Many of my fellow scientists are experimenting with it. Recently Hans Christian Oersted (from Denmark) discovered that if you put a compass next to a wire carrying electricity, it makes the compass needle* turn around. I thought I could take the idea one step further and make a simple **electric motor**. And I was right!

Motors, motors everywhere

Faraday's electric motor was one of the most important inventions of all time. Hundreds of modern machines, from DVD players and electric toothbrushes to electric cars, such as the one shown right, are powered by electric motors.

Timeline

1820 Hans Christian Oersted discovers that a wire with electricity flowing in it forms a magnet

1821 Michael Faraday shows how an electric motor works

* a compass needle is a tiny magnet

HOW AN ELECTRIC MOTOR WORKS   Michael Faraday

You will need:

- a metal dish containing mercury (mercury is a metal that is liquid at room temperature)
- a bar magnet (placed in the centre of the dish)
- a piece of wire hanging loosely with its bottom end in the mercury
- a battery with one **terminal** connected to the hanging wire and the other terminal connected to the metal dish

You should see:

- The bottom end of the hanging wire moves in a circle around and around the magnet

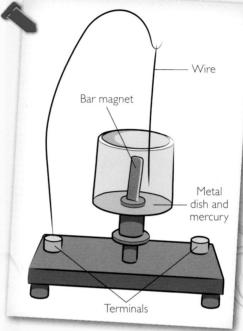

Wire

Bar magnet

Metal dish and mercury

Terminals

How it works:

1 Electricity flows from the battery along the hanging wire, through the mercury and back to the battery.

2 The wire becomes a magnet. Because it is a magnet, the central magnet pushes and pulls on it, making it move in a circle.

1837 The first working electric motor is made. It is used for powering machines in factories

1908 James Murray Spangler (USA) uses an electric motor to power the first domestic **vacuum** cleaner

A CALCULATOR MACHINE

INVENTOR: CHARLES BABBAGE

This inventing business is very frustrating! I've spent years designing machines that can do sums, but I still haven't managed to build one. I call them calculating machines and I'm sure they will be used everywhere one day.

DID YOU KNOW?

Babbage was often ill when he was a child, and spent a lot of time at home. His parents once told his teachers not to "tax his brain too much"!

Charles Babbage

TIMELINE

1821	Charles Babbage began designing his first calculating machine
1833	Babbage designs a new machine – far more advanced than the first because Babbage wanted it to carry out complicated sums
1871	Babbage dies without building either of his machines

PARTS OF A CALCULATOR MACHINE Charles Babbage

1 A punched-card* reader. Some cards contain data (information) and some contain instructions.

2 A section that does additions and subtractions (sums), known as the mill.

3 A store where the results of the sums done in the mill are stored to be used later.

4 A printing section where results are printed on to paper.

5 A steam engine to power the machine.

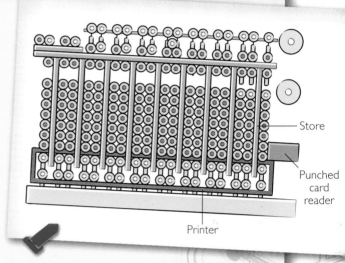

Store

Punched card reader

Printer

Babbage's failure

Charles Babbage's machines would have contained thousands of **cogs**, **levers**, and other small parts. At the time these would have been tricky and very costly to make. This was one reason why Babbage never built the machines.

1938 Konrad Zuse (Germany) builds the first electric computer

1991 The London Science Museum completes Babbage's calculating machine

---

* the punched-card contains information for the machine

THE ELECTRIC LIGHT BULB

INVENTOR: THOMAS ALVA EDISON

Thomas Alva Edison

I've spent my whole life inventing things. I've become famous for it. I've come up with new types of telegraph machine, a microphone, and the world's first machine for recording sound. But my most famous invention is the electric light bulb. What a bright idea that was!

Thomas Alva Edison

Edison v Swan

Most people believe that Edison invented the light bulb, shown right. But it was also invented in Britain by Joseph Swan. At first Edison and Swan argued over who should be granted the patent for the light bulb, but in 1883 they began manufacturing bulbs together.

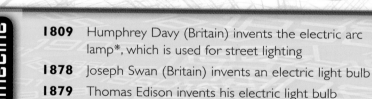

TIMELINE

1809 Humphrey Davy (Britain) invents the electric arc lamp*, which is used for street lighting

1878 Joseph Swan (Britain) invents an electric light bulb

1879 Thomas Edison invents his electric light bulb

* an arc lamp produced light from a powerful electrical spark

THE ELECTRIC LIGHT BULB   Thomas Edison

Glass bulb

Filament

Terminals

The Edison light bulb has the following parts:

1. Filament

A thin thread of **carbonized** bamboo (made by heating thin strips of bamboo without letting it burn). When electricity flows through the **filament**, it makes the filament so hot that it glows brightly. The filament is held in place by thin wires that carry electricity to it.

2. Glass bulb

The air is sucked out of a thin glass container. This makes a vacuum. The vacuum stops the filament burning up (which would happen if there was air in the container).

3. Terminals

The terminals on the outside of the bulb are connected to the filament. They carry electricity in and out of the bulb.

1881	Edison builds an electricity **generating station** in New York to produce electricity for light bulbs in the city
1883	Edison and Swan join forces to make electric light bulbs
1926	Edmund Germer (Germany) invents the **fluorescent** light bulb
1990s	Energy-saving bulbs are introduced to replace filament light bulbs

THE TELEPHONE

INVENTOR: ALEXANDER GRAHAM BELL

It's true that I invented the telephone, but I was helped along by a lucky accident. I was experimenting with a new type of **telegraph** machine for sending **Morse code** messages when I heard sounds coming from it. It was incredible! This spurred me on to make a machine to send voices along a telegraph wire.

DID YOU KNOW?

In later life Bell refused to have a telephone in the study where he worked. He thought the telephone's ringing was a nuisance!

The telephone made staying in touch much easier for people.

Alexander Graham Bell

TIMELINE		
1875	Alexander Graham Bell sends sounds along a telegraph wire	
1876	Bell builds the very first working telephone	
1876	Elisha Grey (USA) also designs a working telephone	
1876	Bell is awarded a patent for his telephone	

EXPERIMENTAL TELEPHONE Alexander Graham Bell

You will need:

Parts for the **transmitter**:

- Paper cone
- Diaphragm*
- Needle attached to diaphragm
- Metal dish containing **acid**
- Battery

Parts for the receiver:

- **Electromagnet**
- Metal reed

How it works:

1 The battery pushes electricity through the needle, the acid, and the dish. Then the electricity flows along a wire to the electromagnet in the **receiver** and back along another wire to the battery.

2 Speaking into the transmitter makes the diaphragm move up and down. This makes the tip of the needle move up and down in the acid. In turn this makes the electricity flowing to the receiver weaker or stronger.

3 At the receiver the electricity changes how strongly the electromagnet pulls on the metal plate. This makes the metal plate vibrate up and down, creating sound.

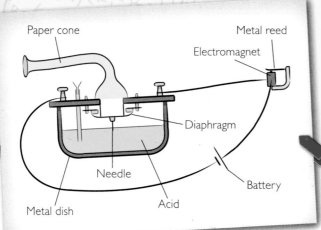

Paper cone

Metal reed

Electromagnet

Diaphragm

Needle

Acid

Battery

Metal dish

1878	The first **telephone exchange** is opened in Connecticut, USA
1891	Almon Strowger (USA) invents the automatic telephone exchange (which allows callers to dial other people)
1971	The first mobile telephone network is opened in Finland

* a thin, flexible sheet of metal

THE WIRELESS TELEGRAPH

INVENTOR: GUGLIELMO MARCONI

Guglielmo Marconi

I've just heard my brother's shotgun fire. That was his signal to let me know he received my wireless telegraph message. It means my invention is working. I've managed to send a message using radio waves!

DID YOU KNOW?

Radio communications quickly became popular on ships for keeping in contact with the shore and other ships. As the *Titanic* sank in the Atlantic in 1912, radio operators on board sent distress signals using Marconi equipment.

The Titanic sent out a call for help using Morse code.

TIMELINE

1888	Heinrich Hertz (Germany) discovers radio waves
1895	Guglielmo Marconi sends messages using radio waves
1899	Marconi sends radio signals across the English Channel, between England and France

COMMUNICATION WITHOUT WIRES — Guglielmo Marconi

How it works:

The transmitter
- Sends out radio waves when its Morse code key is pressed down.
- A transmitter is made up of an aerial (a long wire or metal plate held in the air) connected to a special electric **circuit**.
- Inside the circuit a spark creates a powerful surge of electricity in the aerial. This sends radio waves.

The receiver
- Also made up of an aerial, like the transmitter. Picks up radio waves from the transmitter.
- When radio waves hit the aerial they create electricity. The receiver's electric circuit picks up this electricity and sends it to a bell, making it ring.

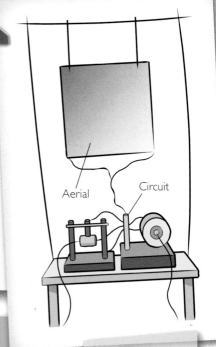

Aerial   Circuit

This diagram shows a radio transmitter.

A family business

Marconi began his experiments in his family's large home in Italy. Marconi's father thought he was wasting his time, but his mother gave him money to buy equipment, and his brother became his assistant.

1901	Marconi sends a radio signal across the Atlantic from England to Canada using 60-metre (197 ft) aerials
1906	The first successful transmission of music by radio
1920s	The first radio stations are **broadcasting**
1930s	Television broadcasting by radio signals

THE VACUUM CLEANER

Inventor: James Murray Spangler

I've been a furniture salesman and an inventor, but recently I've worked sweeping carpets in a department store. I suffer from asthma, and the dust from the carpets made me cough really badly. I was so fed up that I decided to make an electric carpet-cleaning machine.

DID YOU KNOW?

Hoover's vacuum's were so successful that Hoover is now often used as another word for a vacuum cleaner. Perhaps instead of "hoovering", we should say "spangling"!

Vacuum cleaners make cleaning easier and less time-consuming.

Timeline

1901 Hubert Cecil Booth (UK) builds a horse-drawn, petrol-driven vacuum cleaner that sucks dust through hoses

1907 James Murray Spangler invents a portable vacuum cleaner

THE 'SUCTION SWEEPER' James Murray Spangler

1 Take a manual carpet sweeper with a rotating brush. Cut a hole in the back of the case.

2 Find an electric motor (for example, the motor from an electric sewing machine).

3 Put a fan on the shaft of the motor. Mount the motor on the carpet sweeper so that the fan sucks air out of the carpet sweeper case.

4 Place a leather belt around the shaft of the motor and the shaft of the sweeper's spinning brush.

5 Attach a pillow case to the sweeper so that air from the fan is blown into it (the bag acts as a filter, allowing air to escape, but trapping dust).

6 Finally, add a broom handle to push the sweeper along.

Testing: switch on the motor and push the sweeper forwards. The brush should spin and dust-filled air should be blown into the bag.

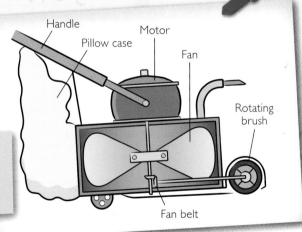

Spangler's prototype carpet cleaner

Handle · Pillow case · Motor · Fan · Rotating brush · Fan belt

1908 William Hoover (USA) begins manufacturing Spangler's vacuum cleaners

1983 James Dyson (UK) launches the world's first bagless vacuum cleaner, which removes dust from the air by spinning it at high speed

A FLYING MACHINE

INVENTORS: ORVILLE WRIGHT AND WILBUR WRIGHT

Phew! Orville (my brother) has just brought our aircraft *Flyer* safely back to the ground. We've just made the first-ever successful flight in an aeroplane. Today is December 17, 1903. Remember this date! Now it's my turn to be the pilot...

A long road to success

The Wright brothers' success came from carrying out thousands of flight tests with kites and gliders over a period of four years before attempting to build their powered aircraft. Rival **aviators** took short cuts and failed.

Orville Wright (top) and Wilbur Wright (bottom)

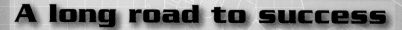

timeline

1901	The Wrights complete their Glider number 3
1903	Orville Wright makes the first powered, controlled flight of a heavier-than-air aircraft at Kitty Hawk, North Carolina, USA

A GUIDE TO THE FLYER   Wilbur Wright

- The wings are made up of a wooden frame covered with cloth. The curved shape of the wing creates lift* as *Flyer* moves forwards.
- A lightweight engine drives two **propellers**, one on each wing, via chains. Propeller speed is managed by the engine's **throttle** control.
- Flight direction is controlled by moveable surfaces. These consist of:
  - rudders at the rear that turn *Flyer*
  - elevators at the front that make *Flyer* climb and descend
  - wing tips that twist to make *Flyer* roll from side to side

- Levers linked to the rudders, elevators, and wing tips allow the pilot to move these surfaces to control *Flyer*.
  - the take-off system consists of a trolley on a rail. Skids are provided for landing.

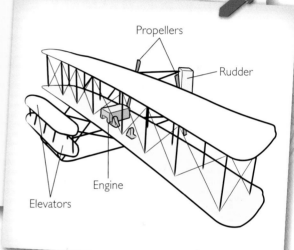

Propellers

Rudder

Engine

Elevators

1905   Flyer III is the first practical aircraft, capable of long flights

1969   The first flight of the Boeing 747. Its **fuselage** is longer than the Wright's first historic flight

* an upwards push that keeps *Flyer* in the air

THE TELEVISION

INVENTOR: JOHN LOGIE BAIRD

I've invented air-cushioned shoes and a glass razor. Unfortunately, the shoes burst and the razor shattered! But I'd always loved the idea of transmitting moving pictures of events. So, in 1925 I built the world's first working television. Amazing! Here's how it worked ...

Today, everyone can watch television because of Baird's invention.

TV history

The first television receivers were huge, but had tiny screens, just a few centimetres wide. Early televisions such as this one (right) look very old fashioned today.

TIMELINE

1925	John Logie Baird builds a television system that sends a moving image
1926	Baird demonstrates his television system in Selfridges department store in London
1928	Baird sends a television signal from London to New York

HOW THE TELEVISION WORKS   John Logie Baird

The system uses a transmitter to send pictures and a receiver to display them.

The Transmitter

1 Bright light is shone on subject.

2 Motor powers spinning disc.

3 Light shining on subject passes through spinning disc. Holes divide the light into lines. This process is known as scanning.

4 Light then hits photovoltaic cell*, which reacts by sending out an electrical signal.

5 A transmitter turns the electrical signals into radio signals.

6 The signals spread through the air.

The Receiver

7 The aerial turns radio signals into an electrical signal.

8 The signal controls the brightness of a light bulb.

9 The light from the bulb shines through the spinning disc, recreating the lines of the picture.

10 The picture appears on a small glass screen.

> **This diagram shows a television transmitter.**

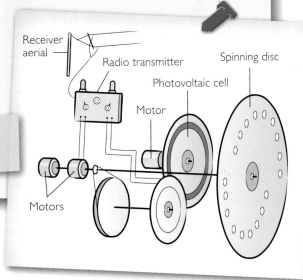

Receiver aerial

Radio transmitter

Spinning disc

Photovoltaic cell

Motor

Motors

1929   The British Broadcasting Corporation begins to broadcast television programmes using Baird's equipment

1950s   Colour television broadcasts begin

* a photovoltaic cell is sensitive to light

THE ROCKET

INVENTOR: ROBERT GODDARD

Robert Goddard

As a child I used to dream of amazing vehicles that could take me to the stars. Today, after five years of experiments, I tested my first rocket, and zoom... up it went. I hope it's the first step on the journey to space.

DID YOU KNOW?

Not many people believed that Goddard's rockets would work. How wrong they were – today, Goddard is known as the father of the space age.

Goddard's work made possible all later explorations into space.

TIMELINE

1150 In China, the first gunpowder-fuelled rockets are used as weapons

1926 In the USA, Robert Goddard launches the first successful liquid-fuelled rocket

NOTES ON A LIQUID-FUELLED ROCKET   Robert Goddard

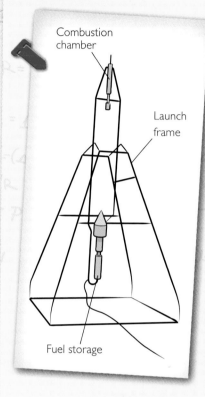

Combustion chamber

Launch frame

Fuel storage

Use of liquid fuel

1 The flow of liquid to the engine can be adjusted, so the thrust* of the rocket can be controlled.

2 I've decided to use petrol and liquid oxygen as the fuels.

Fuel storage

1 Fuel is stored in tanks at the base of the rocket, petrol in one and liquid oxygen in the other.

2 A small heater turns the liquid oxygen to gas.

3 Pipes transport fuel up to the **combustion chamber**. These also form the frame of the rocket.

Combustion chamber

1 Valves allow petrol and oxygen to mix in the combustion chamber.

2 The petrol burns and produces hot gases that rush out through the **nozzle**.

Launch frame

The rocket is supported before it launches by a metal launch frame.

1942   Germany launches V2 rockets against Britain

1957   A rocket lifts the first satellite, Sputnik 1, into orbit around the Earth

1969   A Saturn V rocket launches the astronauts to the first Moon landings

* the push made by a rocket engine

THE JET ENGINE
INVENTOR: FRANK WHITTLE

I used to be a fighter pilot so I knew a jet engine would let a plane fly higher and faster. I finally built a working **prototype** jet engine, but then ran out of cash. At first the government didn't take my engine seriously. But when war with Germany looked on the cards in 1939, they stumped up the cash to help me build it.

DID YOU KNOW?

Frank Whittle was a fighter pilot, flying instructor, and test pilot in the British Royal Air Force. He was once struck off from a flying competition for flying dangerously to show off his skills.

Modern jet fighter planes are based on Whittle's work.

TIMELINE

1937 Hans von Ohain (Germany) tests an experimental jet engine

1937 Frank Whittle tests his model jet engine, called the WU

1939 The first flight of a jet-powered aircraft, the Heinkel 178, powered by von Ohain's engine

A GUIDE TO THE JET ENGINE Frank Whittle

1 Air intake
Collects air needed for fuel to burn.

2 Compressor
A high-speed spinning fan sucks air through the intake and squeezes it.

3 Combustion chamber
The air flows into the combustion chamber. Fuel is also injected into the chamber. The fuel burns, creating super-hot gases.

4 Turbine
Gases from the combustion chamber rush through sets of blades, making them spin. The **turbine** drives the compressor (see 2 above).

5 Exhaust
Hot gases blast out of engine here.

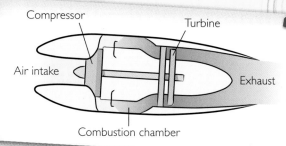

Compressor   Turbine

Air intake

Exhaust

Combustion chamber

Whittle and von Ohain

Both Whittle and von Ohain rushed to perfect their fighter plane engines, but in the end jet fighters like the one shown right played only a minor part in WWII.

1941   First flight of an aircraft (the Gloster E28) powered by Whittle's jet engine

1949   The first jet-powered passenger plane, the de Havilland Comet, takes to the air

THE WORLD WIDE WEB

INVENTOR: TIM BERNERS-LEE

Working as a scientist back in the 1980s I used to look at hundreds of documents stored on computers. One day I realized how useful it would be to jump from one document to another simply by clicking on some sort of link in the document. The end result was the World Wide Web!

Tim Berners-Lee

DID YOU KNOW?

Tim Berners-Lee is now head of the World Wide Web Consortium (W3C), the international organization that controls the World Wide Web. He never made any money from inventing the World Wide Web.

TIMELINE

1969 US Government computers are linked together to share information. This computer network became known as ARPANET

1970s The Internet was born when various other networks around the world were linked to ARPANET

WORLD WIDE WEB FAQS*   Tim Berners-Lee

What is the World Wide Web?

A huge collection of information stored on computers on the Internet (see below) in the form of web pages. The information is in the form of text, images, video, sounds, and other data*.

What is html?

Hypertext mark-up language (html) is a computer language used to build web pages.

What is a link?

A hypertext link is a piece of text or an image on a web page that a user clicks on to go to another web page.

What's needed to look at web pages?

A computer needs software to fetch and display html files. This is called a web browser.

What is the Internet?

A vast computer network made up of millions of computers around the world connected together.

1989	Tim Berners-Lee develops hypertext mark-up language
1991	The World Wide Web is launched on the Internet
2008	The number of web pages on the Internet reaches one trillion

* originally it was just text

GLOSSARY

acid liquid that can rot materials

aviators people who fly or build aircraft

broadcasting sending signals from one transmitter to many different receivers

carbonized turned to carbon

circuit loop electricity flows through

cogs wheels with a rim of teeth

combustion chamber space where fuel burns

electric motor device that turns electricity into movement

electromagnet magnet made by sending electricity through a wire

electron microscope microscope that makes pictures of objects using tiny particles called electrons

filament thin object, like a thread

fluorescent light bulb containing glowing chemicals that give out light

fuselage main part of an aircraft

generating station place where electricity is made

lenses pieces of glass or plastic which bend light rays from an object

levers rods that can pivot up and down or from side to side

micro-organisms plants and animals that are so small you can't see them without using a microscope

microscope device used to look in detail at tiny objects

Morse code code in which letters are shown by dots and dashes

nozzle hole that gas comes out of

propellers fan-shaped objects that spin to push or pull an aircraft

prototype early working version of something

receiver device that turns signals back into sound

technology scientific information that tells people how to build or make something

telegraph machine that sends written messages using electricity

telephone exchange place where telephone lines from different houses are connected together

terminal one of the two metal connections on battery

throttle handle that controls the speed of an engine

transmitter device that turns sound into an electrical signal

turbine set of fans that spin at high speed when gas rushes past them

vacuum place where there is nothing, not even air

FURTHER INFORMATION

WEBSITES

The Thomas Edison National Historical Park, New Jersey has lots of information about Edison. You can find the website at:
www.nps.gov/edis/index.htm

Read more about the Wright Brothers on the official website at:
http://wrightbrothers.info

There is an interactive site about Marconi at:
www.marconicalling.com

BOOKS

The Story of Inventions by Anna Claybourne and Adam Larkum. Usborne (2007).

The Way Things Work by David Macauley and Neil Ardley. Dorling Kindersley (2004).

How Nearly Everything was Invented by the Brainwaves by Ralph Lazar and Lisa Swerling. Dorling Kindersley (2008).

Wow! Inventions that Changed the World by Philip Ardagh. Pan MacMillan (2006).

PLACES TO VISIT

The Science Museum
South Kensington, London
Exhibits include a Babbage machine and Baird's television
www.sciencemuseum.org.uk

Musuem of Science and Industry
Liverpool Road, Manchester
www.mosi.org.uk

INDEX

acid 15
aircraft 20–21, 26–27
aviators 20

Babbage, Charles 10–11
Baird, John Logie 22–23
battery 9, 15
Bell, Alexander Graham 14–15
Berners-Lee, Tim 28–29

calculator 10–11
carbonized 13
circuit 17
cogs 11
combustion chamber 25, 27
computers 11, 27, 28–29

da Vinci, Leonardo 5

Edison, Thomas Alva 12–13
electric light bulb 12–13, 23
electric motor 8–9, 19
electricity 8–9, 12–13, 15, 17, 23
electromagnet 15
engines 11, 21, 26–27

Faraday, Michael 8–9
filament 13
fluorescent 13
fuselage 21

generating station 13
Goddard, Robert 24–25

html 29
Hoover, William 18, 19

jet engine 26–27

lenses 6, 7
lever 11

Marconi, Guglielmo 16–17
microscope 6–7
Morse code 14, 17

nozzle 25

patent 5, 12, 14
propellers 21
prototype 26

radio signals/waves 16–17, 23
receiver 15, 17, 22, 23
rocket 24–25

sketches 5
Spangler, James Murray 18–19
steam engine 11

technology 5
telegraph 14, 16–17
telephone 14–15
television 22–23
terminal 9
throttle 21
transmitter 15, 17, 23
turbine 27

vacuum 13
vacuum cleaner 9, 18–19
van Leeuwenhoek, Anton 6–7

Whittle, Frank 26–27
World Wide Web 28–29
Wright brothers 20–21